HAND.

~ 101 ~
Uses for an Old
John Deere

By Cletus Hohman

Voyageur Press

A TOWN SQUARE GIFTBOOK

Edited by Cletus Hohman
Designed by JoDee Turner
Printed in Hong Kong

02   03   04   05   06   5   4   3   2   1

Library of Congress Cataloging-in-Publication Data

Hohman, Cletus.
    101 uses for an old John Deere / [captions] by Cletus Hohman.
      p.cm.
    ISBN 0-89658-606-5 (hardcover)
    1. Tractors—Humor. 2. John Deere tractors—Humor. I. Title: One
hundred one uses for an old John Deere. II. Title.
    PN6231.T677 H64 2002
    818'.602—dc21

                                        2002002645

Published by Voyageur Press, Inc.
123 North Second Street, P.O. Box 338, Stillwater, MN 55082 U.S.A.
651-430-2210, fax 651-430-2211
books@voyageurpress.com
www.voyageurpress.com

Acknowledgments

Our thanks to all who helped bring this book to life: John O. Allen of J. C. Allen & Son; Keith Baum; Tom Benda of Apple Creek Publishing; Andy Kraushaar; and Paul Rezendes.

Cover photo © Keith Baum

On the endpapers: 1930s John Deere humorous postcard.

Page 1: On the frontispiece: John Deere advertising painting by artist Walter Haskell Hinton. (Deere & Company)

Page 2: A lineup of John Deere Model A tractors dating from 1934 to 1938. Owners: Howard and Bonnie Miller. (Photograph © Andy Kraushaar)

Page 3: A youngster tries out the latest John Deere at the Minnesota State Fair.

∾ Contents ∾

A restored John Deere Model GP. (Photograph by Hans Halberstadt)

Matters of Growing Up

1

High Chair

A budding John Deere enthusiast checks out the ergonomics of the latest Deere model at the Minnesota State Fair's Machinery Hill in the 1950s.

Playmate

Iowa artist Charles H. Freitag captured the early appeal of John Deeres in his painting *Autumn Memories*, which features two children at play with their Deere pedal tractor while their parents do farmwork work with their grown-up Deere. (Apple Creek Publishing)

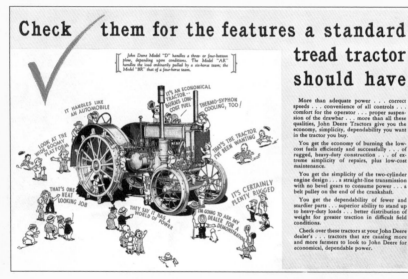

Jungle Gym

Reminiscent of *Gulliver's Travels*, miniscule farm folk crawl all over a John Deere Model D in this 1930s brochure. (Deere & Company)

PINT-SIZED SHADOW

Many a farmer has a pint-sized shadow that tags him everywhere . . . that mimics whatever he says or does. Naturally, the little fellow has his heart set on being a farmer just like his dad.

Modern time-, labor-, and money-saving John Deere power equipment helps childish dreams like this to come true.

Career Planner

A youngster follows Pa's lead in oiling his toy John Deere's Roll-O-Matic front end in this 1949 Deere advertising image. (Deere & Company)

Little Helper

Junior—and the family's trusty John Deere Model D—help out Pa with the farmyard chores in this Charles Freitag painting entitled *Daddy's Little Helper*. (Apple Creek Publishing)

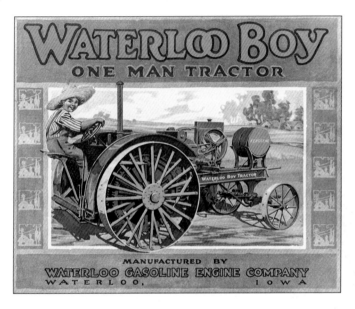

Big Wheel

While piloting his or her tricycle, every farm kid dreamed of driving the family's Waterloo Boy, as shown in this Waterloo Gasoline Engine Company ad. (Deere & Company)

Lego Set

Down on the farm, Tinker Toys, Meccano, and Lego sets were not needed—
real tractors were more fun to work on. (Deere & Company)

8

Goal Posts

The exhaust pipes on a John Deere Model D were just right for kicking field goals in a friendly game of football. (Photograph by Hans Halberstadt)

9

Childhood Pal

You never forget your childhood pals, whether it's your brother or your family's faithful John Deere Model A. (Photograph © J. C. Allen & Son)

10

Hiding Place

When chores needed doing or when there was a blueberry pie to snitch, the John Deere made a perfect hiding place, as in Charles Freitag's painting *The Barn Raising*. (Apple Creek Publishing)

Teaching Tool

When things went wrong with your John Deere—of any size or model—the Deere dealership was the first stop for parts and a helping hand, as in this painting by Walter Haskell Hinton. (Deere & Company)

Anatomy Lesson

The young folk learned the mysteries of life and how a tractor worked from this cutaway John Deere 4010. (Photograph by Chester Peterson Jr.)

Showing pulley side of the new John Deere Model "H" Tractor. Belt pulley is standard equipment.

Dream Machine

Every farm kid dreamed of someday being big enough to take the wheel of the family's John Deere Model H. (Deere & Company)

14

School Bus

Painted yellow and mounted with a cab, John Deere's Model AI Industrial tractor looked the part of the rural school bus. Owners: Lester, Kenny, and Harland Layher. (Photograph © Andy Kraushaar)

15

Rite of Passage

Driving the family's Deere was a big responsibility—and a rite of passage for many a farm youth, as shown in this 1940s Deere ad. (Deere & Company)

16

Flight Simulator

If they couldn't drive tractor, every kid dreamed of at least growing up to be a pilot and flying an airplane. Sometimes a John Deere was the best flight simulator. (Deere & Company)

Character Builder

It was no secret that after the intial flush of excitement of driving tractor had worn off, there were long hours to be spent behind that steering wheel. (Photograph © J. C. Allen & Son)

18

Family Pet

The whole gang gathers around its 1939 John Deere Model H, making it feel as if it is part of the family. Owner: Allen Martin. (Photograph © Keith Baum)

19

Driver's Ed Vehicle

20

First Car

Tractors were often a first car for farm youths—although they were rarely allowed to drive the machines far from the fields that needed plowing. This classic image that appeared on Deere brochures and calendars was painted by Walter Haskell Hinton. (Deere & Company)

21 ——————————

Object of Desire

When Deere's Models A and B got a styling facelift by noted designer Henry Drefyuss in 1938, the tractors became an object of desire for all.

23

Guy Magnet

Nothing made a fashion statement for the well-dressed farm girl like the new
John Deere. No woman could resist a Deere tractor—and no man could resist
a woman with a Deere, as pictured in this painting by artist Walter Haskell
Hinton. (Deere & Company)

Babe Magnet

The latest John Deere Model A was the ideal machine to catch the eye of that certain special lady.

Hot Date

Few dates were as romantic as a trip to the local fair's Machinery Hill to check out the latest and greatest in John Deere tractors.

26

Ride to Lover's Lane

John Deere Model AO was an ideal way to make the trip to Lover's Lane in style. (Photograph by Hans Halberstadt)

Wedding Present

Those that farm together—with a John Deere tractor—stay together. (Minnesota Historical Society)

28

Honeymoon Cruise

With your Waterloo Boy–Overtime tractor, a honeymoon could be full of romance—and you could get some plowing done at the same time.

Matters of Everyday Life

29

Coffee Bar

The John Deere Model 60 made an ideal coffee bar while waiting for the harvest to come in, as in this painting by Charles Freitag entitled *Bumper Crop*. (Apple Creek Publishing)

Volkswagen Bug

The diminutive John Deere Model LA was the Volkswagen Bug of the Deere line. (Photograph by Hans Halberstadt)

Cadillac

You traveled in style when you drove a John Deere Model AW.

Lamborghini

Swoopy aerodynamics and curvaceous bodywork made the John Deere Model 620 Orchard a stylish machine. And at speed, Deere's orchard machines and Lamborghinis could sometimes be confused—even by seasoned old-timers. This was Ertl's limited-edition Expo 2 model of the 620-O.

Hot Rod

Deere engineer C. H. Melvin's tractor plow prototype was a true hot rod among tractors with its macho big wheels. (Deere & Company)

Muscle Car

"Muscle" was the perfect word to describe the John Deere Model 830 Diesel.
(Photograph by Chester Peterson Jr.)

Company Car

The dapper businessman would have been proud to be seen on Deere engineer Max Sklovsky's B-2 tractor prototype. (Deere & Company)

Dragster

Fitted with rollbar and front weights, the John Deere 4020 looked the part of a top-fuel dragster. With its big rear wheels and powerful New Generation four-cylinder engine, the 4020 could beat many a challenger in a drag race to the fenceline. (Photograph by Chester Peterson Jr.)

Convertible

Cadillac ragtops and convertible '57 Chevys had nothing on tractors when it came to top-down motoring on a sunny summer day. A John Deere Model BW was the ideal way to ride in style through the fields. (Photograph by Hans Halberstadt)

ART HEGGE
JOHN DEERE FARM EQUIPMENT
Sales — Service
Telephone 31 — Westby, Wisconsin

Pickup Truck

A John Deere could handle any load, as shown in this painting by Walter
Haskell Hinton. (Deere & Company)

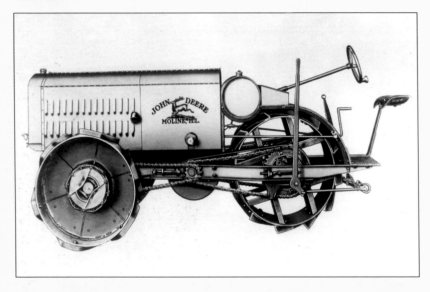

Steam Roller

With its wide wheels, Joseph Dain's John Deere All-Wheel-Drive tractor was
an ideal steam roller. (Deere & Company)

Taxi

Need a cab? You couldn't miss the bright yellow of John Deere's Model DI Industrial amongst the traffic on a busy street. (Photograph © Andy Kraushaar)

Minivan

When the kids were growing and the family station wagon became too cramped, John Deere's 4700 could double as the perfect minivan. (Deere & Company)

Main Street Cruiser

Cruising main street was always a joy on the family's John Deere. And, when challenged to a friendly drag race with rivals, as shown in this painting by Charles Freitag entitled *Friendly Rivals*, you could always count on a Deere. (Apple Creek Publishing)

James Bond 007 Spy Vehicle

Secret agent James Bond 007 could dispense with his Aston Martin sports car in favor of the stealthy John Deere 3020 Orchard, which boasted the latest gadgetry for all farmyard spies. (Deere & Company)

Monster Truck

John Deere's 8020 could crush anything in its path. (Photograph by Chester Peterson Jr.)

HUMVEE

The army's Hummer replaced the venerable Jeep, but John Deere's 9420T can go anywhere a Hummer goes.

Charles Freitag

46 ——

Snowmobile

Each snow fall brought an opportunity to make snowmen, and the John Deere was always nearby to lend a helping hand, as in this Charles Freitag painting. (Apple Creek Publishing)

Indianapolis 500 Race Car

The Indy 500 would never be the same after a lap by John Deere's aerodynamic
Model BO. (Photograph by Hans Halberstadt)

48

Tank

John Deere's 8400T made the ideal secret weapon in keeping the world safe for democracy. (Deere & Company)

Sport Utility Vehicle

Even if you never drove it off road or ever got it dirty, John Deere's 6910S had all the rough and rugged capabilities of a suburbanite's SUV. (Deere & Company)

50
Stealth Fighter

51

UFO

The low-flying capability and slippery streamlining of the John Deere Model 60 Orchard help it elude radar. In low light, such as when it returned from fieldwork at dusk, the 60-O could easily be mistaken for a UFO—which may have been the source of those rumored alien sightings. (Photograph by Andy Kraushaar)

Moon Buggy

Do away with NASA's $200 toilet seats and $50 hammers: John Deere's 8120 could be the perfect lunar exploration vehicle for the space program on a tight budget. (Deere & Company)

Grocery Cart

When the groceries needed getting, John Deere's 950 was the ideal machine—even when Junior tried his hands at the wheel. (Deere & Company)

Extension Ladder

With John Deere's 3800 Telehandler, finally just one farmer was needed to change a light bulb. (Deere & Company)

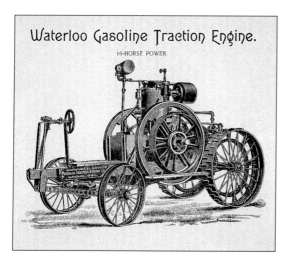

55

Spinning Wheel

56

Oil Rig

When the new, updated John Deere models hit the field, engineer John Froelich's pioneering tractor and Deere forerunner could have a comfortable retirement as a spinning wheel or oil-drilling rig—assuming you had some of the black gold on your back forty. (Deere & Company)

57

Picnic Site

When lunch finally arrived after a long morning in the harvest field, wherever the John Deere stopped made the perfect picnic spot, as in this painting by Walter Haskell Hinton. (Deere & Company)

Lunch Counter

The rear wheel of the John Deere made a perfect lunch counter while Junior and Rover pretended they were Pa cultivating corn, in this famous painting by Walter Haskell Hinton. (Deere & Company)

59

Posture Builder

You learned quickly how to sit up straight and tall in the cast-iron seats of the early John Deere Model A. (Deere & Company)

The New
JOHN DEERE *Model "A"*
GENERAL PURPOSE TRACTOR
with **ADJUSTABLE TREAD**

JOHN DEERE GENERAL PURPOSE

·and One-Man Working Equipment Built for Use on Southern Farms·

Mr. Universe Muscle Builder

Charles Atlas look out! Many a farm youth built muscles the hard way—by spinning the flywheel on a John Deere Model D to start the engine. (Library of Congress)

61

Beach Chair

62

Patio Furniture

When the going got rough, the right place to be was at the beach. John Deere engineer Walter Silver's motor cultivator prototype made an ideal beach chair or patio lounger—complete with an umbrella to shade you from the sun. (Deere & Company)

Exercise Bike

Who needs an exercise bicycle when you have a John Deere Model 60 pedal tractor? And, when it is mounted with a plow, you can get some work done while getting a workout. (Photograph © Keith Baum)

64

La-Z-Boy

When the day was done, the hood of your John Deere made a fine place to put your feet up. (Library of Congress)

Sunday Drive

The John Deere was the ideal vehicle for a Sunday drive—but everyone always hurried home when the dinner bell rang. Artist Walter Haskell Hinton's painting captured the farmwife's call to the table. (Deere & Company)

Dog Walker

Why bother walking when a John Deere can take you anywhere Fido needed to go? (Minnesota Historical Society)

67

Portrait Studio

The John Deere was as much a part of the family as the prize-winning steer and appeared in many a family picture. (Deere & Company)

68

Mother-in-Law Apartment

69

Guest Room

The mammoth wheels of a John Deere tractor make an ideal spare room when unexpected—or unwanted—guests come to call.

Lawn Ornament

Nothing said class like a John Deere 2510 lawn ornament. (Photograph by Chester Peterson Jr.)

Guard Dog

With its bulldog-like stance, John Deere's 8010 is guaranteed to keep burglars away. (Photograph by Chester Peterson Jr.)

72

Four-Wheel-Drive Mud Buggy

73

Insurance Claim

When the John Deere Model D met its match in mud, it was time to collect on all the money you had been paying that slick-talking insurance salesman. (Glenbow Archives)

Fertilizer

Rust to dust and old Johnny Poppers to ashes—at some point an old tractor becomes fertilizer, rusting back into the earth from which it came. (Photograph by Hans Halberstadt)

Junk Pile Starter Kit

To some folk, the rusting hulk of an old John Deere got the heart racing. The same sight made others wring their hands. (Photograph by Hans Halberstadt)

❧ Matters of Fun ❧

76

Star of the Show

77

Petting Zoo

The John Deere tent was always one of the main draws at the county or state fair as everyone stopped by to kick some tires. For young and old alike, the lineup of new John Deeres was a veritable petting zoo. (Photograph © J. C. Allen & Son)

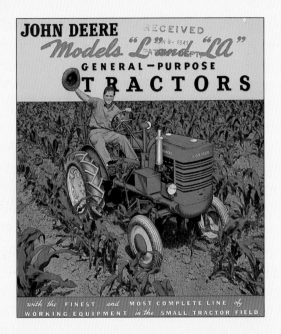

Joy Ride

Some folk drive a Corvette, others a Cadillac, but a John Deere Model LA is always guaranteed to put a smile on a farmer's face. (Deere & Company)

Tilt-A-Whirl

Ready for the ride of your life? John Deere's 6010 Series with its tilt cab was just the thing after the county fair shut down for the season. (Deere & Company)

Sideshow Attraction

Few things attract a crowd of farmers like horsepower, and this county-fair sideshow let them get up close and personal with a John Deere tractor pull. (Photograph © J. C. Allen & Son)

81

Merry-Go-Round

If you drove your John Deere 4450-MFWD around in a circle enough times, even the roughest and toughest farmer was bound to get dizzy. (Deere & Company)

Mechanical Bull

Riding an early tractor, such as the Dain All-Wheel-Drive, with their steel wheels and cast-iron seats, was a challenge in itself. (Deere & Company)

83

Chorus Line

John Deere 8020 tractors, arrayed in a Rockettes-style line, get ready to strut their stuff. (Photograph by Chester Peterson Jr.)

A NEW FARM HAND.

#45 © 1937-

F.D.CONARD

88

Y CITY, KANSAS.

84

Sci-Fi Movie Terror

A grasshopper invasion takes on new meaning in this tall-tale postcard from the 1930s.

85

Super Hero

Move over Superman, Batman, and Spider-Man! There's a new super hero on the prowl, keeping the world safe for the law-abiding common folk: Meet the John Deere Model D. (Deere & Company)

DEPEN

Hundreds of pounds lighter.
Hundreds of parts simpler.
Saves in fuel and oil.

JOH

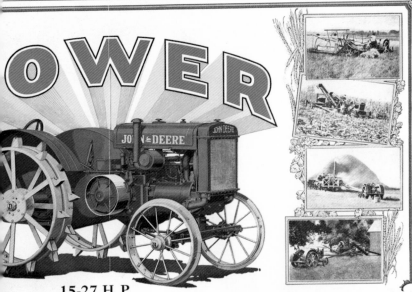

OWER

15-27 H. P.

LE • ECONOMICAL • DURABLE

p cost.

completely enclosed.

automatically oiled.

Simple adjustments easy to make.

Easy to keep in running order.

Easy to get at working parts.

Easier to understand and operate.

Finest materials and workmanship.

Meets every need on the farm.

EERE FARM TRACTOR

86 —

Bird-Watcher's Perch

When spring was in the air and the first robins arrived to sing their song, a tractor seat often made a fine perch for bird watching. (Deere & Company)

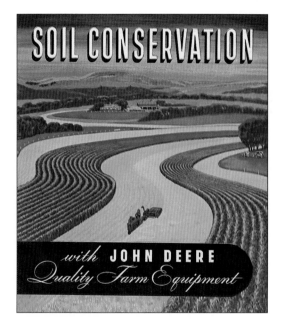

Artist's Paintbrush

With a John Deere tractor and hay chopper, the farmer became an artist with the field as a canvas. (Deere & Company)

Artist's Canvas

Restoring an old tractor is a work of art and of the heart, as depicted in
Charles Freitag's painting *Restoration II*. (Apple Creek Publishing)

89

Christmas Tree

Wrapped in Christmas lights, a John Deere Model 50 is a stirring sight at Yuletide. (Photograph © Paul Rezendes)

Matters of ∞ ∞
Growing Old and Wise

90

First Love

A farmer never forgets his or her first love. (Photograph © J. C. Allen & Son)

Second Husband

The John Deere riding mower is the ideal companion, helping to complete household tasks in a timely manner. (Deere & Company)

Big Boys' Toys

As the saying goes, the bigger the boy, the bigger the toy. And a John Deere 5020 makes a fine toy—especially when fitted with a V-8 engine. (Photograph by Chester Peterson Jr.)

Bragging Rights

Who wouldn't want to brag about their John Deere Model A? Owners: Lester, Kenny, and Harland Layher. (Photograph © Andy Kraushaar)

Trophies

A John Deere 3010 and 4010 make a fine mid-life crisis trophy. Who needs to buy a Harley-Davidson or take up playing the saxophone when you have two such Deeres? (Photograph by Chester Peterson Jr.)

95

Sex Symbol

For raw sex appeal, it was tough to top the John Deere Model A. (Photography © J. C. Allen & Son)

96

Status Symbol

It's hard to keep up with the Jones when they have a collection of five John Deere Model As. Owners: Howard and Bonnie Miller. (Photograph © Andy Kraushaar)

97

A Best Friend

When you worked with your John Deere day after day, year after year, decade after decade, it was hard not to call it "Friend." (Deere & Company)

98

One of the Ties That Bind

The John Deere 4620 was just one of the good things about the farming life. (Photograph by Chester Peterson Jr.)

Walker

As one grows old, it's good to know you can always lean on your John Deere HWH.
(Photograph by Hans Halberstadt)

100

Time Machine

Watching a venerable John Deere Model D still at work transported more than one old-timer back to the good old days. (Deere & Company)

101

Perfect Ending

An old John Deere provided a happy ending to many a story. (Photograph by Hans Halberstadt)